Etsy Business Success

How to make your first $1000 on Etsy without spending a dime

Table of Contents

INTRODUCTION 1

CHAPTER 1 – AN INTRODUCTION TO ETSY 3

CHAPTER 2 – WHY CHOOSE ETSY TO SELL YOUR CRAFTS 7

CHAPTER 3 – CREATING AN ACCOUNT AND SETTING UP YOUR SHOP ON ETSY 15

CHAPTER 4 – HOW TO KEEP YOUR CUSTOMERS SATISFIED AND HAPPY 23

CHAPTER 5 – START SELLING ON ETSY WITHOUT SPENDING A DIME 27

CHAPTER 6 – THINGS THAT SELL WELL ON ETSY 29

CONCLUSION 33

Introduction

I want to thank you and congratulate you for downloading the book, Etsy Business Success.

This book contains proven steps and strategies on how to make your first $1000 on Etsy without spending a dime.

Etsy is the premier e-commerce website where you can sell artistic, crafty, and handmade, and unique manufactured items. This book introduces you to the world of Etsy, tells you about the various benefits it has over other websites, and provides solid reasons on why you should choose it. It also contains step by step guide on how to set up an account on Etsy, how to create a shop there, how to create a listing, etc., and guides you on how to start making money on Etsy without spending a dime. This book serves as a complete and comprehensive guide for beginners and people wanting to create a shop on Etsy.

It also contains tips and tricks for optimizing your product listings for search engines, taking good photos, and keeping your customers happy and satisfied.

Thanks again for downloading this book, I hope you enjoy it!

Chapter 1 – An Introduction to Etsy

Every few years a new website opens up that provides solution to a problem we did not even know we had. For instance, while we have no problem using Facebook and are so addicted to it, a new website called 'Ello' has popped up; it distinguishes itself from all other social networking sites by claiming to be completely free of ads, and promises to remain so. And then we realise how annoying those advertisements had been for us all along. In the same way, while there had been many websites where people could sell stuff online, Etsy came along. It distinguished itself from others by becoming the premier website for selling vintage items, handcrafted goods, and exclusive factory manufactured items.

Etsy is a website that is chiefly recognised as an online shop for arts, crafts, household, vintage, jewellery, and baked goods and items. It does not allow reselling items. Vintage items need to be at least twenty years old to be sold on Etsy. All sellers get their own page on Etsy, like a website, where they can set up their own shop with ease. There is no hassle of setting up payment methods, and it is easier than setting up your own website. There are lots of customisation options for the online shop that can be set up there, so it is really convenient for people to start selling their items on Etsy instead of making their own website. This allows people to focus on their craft instead of having to worry about maintaining and updating a website. It charges only a small fee which becomes negligible when you compare it to the costs of creating and maintaining a website. You can list your items on Etsy for only $0.20 per item. The fee is per item, so if you list 5 items of the same kind, say 5 rings, the total would be $1.

Etsy was launched in June 2005. The e-commerce website has continuously grown since its launch and now boasts over 30 million creative businesses and buyers. It has a lot of promotional tools that allow you to promote your own products. The membership and registration on Etsy is free. A 3.5% fee is taken from each item that is sold. Once an item is listed, it remains there until it is sold, or for up to four months. Etsy frequently introduces changes and updates. It has evolved from an online store to a community and has a style that is more like Facebook, allowing the buyers and sellers to connect with each other, become friends, etc.

In this book, you will learn how to create an account on Etsy, setup your shop, and start selling, along with search engine optimisation to boost your sales, suggestions on items that you should sell, and various other tips and tricks to improve your sales and service and get a 100% customer satisfaction. The more satisfied your customers are, the better your shop will be, and the more money you will make.

Chapter 2 – Why Choose Etsy to Sell Your Crafts

If you search on the Internet, you will find many platforms where you can sell your crafts, products, and items. You have got Amazon, eBay, etc. along with the option to create your very own website, so why choose Etsy? No matter which website you choose to sell your products on, there will always be pros and cons. Etsy, too, might be limiting in some ways but it also comes with a fair amount of benefits. In this chapter we will take a look at the benefits you get if you choose to setup a shop and sell items on Etsy.

A Very Easy Setup and Loads of Customisation Options

One of the main benefits of choosing Etsy to sell your products and items is the easy setup. All you need to do is basically go to the website and register yourself as a seller. From there onwards, you can set your shop up and customise it, including a shop name, logo, shopping sections, etc. It is very easy to add and list products, add photos and descriptions, etc. and start selling them on Etsy. The predesigned templates make the process of listing items very simple and intuitive.

The customisation options it offers includes:

- Custom policies for your store

- Ability to accept payments through credit card and PayPal

- Ability to accept payments through money orders

- Announce Page where you can make announcements or share important information about your store/business

- A shipping calculator for international shipping as well as shipping inside the United States

- Ability to customise shipping options

- An option to offer coupon codes

- Ability to combine different orders from the same customer and ship them as one

Exposure and Traffic

One of the main advantages of opening up your shop on Etsy is that it already has millions of users so you do not have to worry about bringing traffic to your store. On the other hand, if you open a website, you need to do a lot of promotion and even then it is difficult to bring organic traffic to it, but Etsy already has organic traffic, so that will be one less thing for you to worry about. Even when you promote your website through Google ads or some other paid promotion, your website may get more traffic but it will take time to actually get an interested buyer. Since Etsy is already established and home to buyers and sellers alike, the traffic, visitors, and views you get on it are from people who are actually interested in buying your products and could potentially become your regular customers; It has a monthly traffic of 25 million visitors.

Furthermore, Etsy allows you to tweak your product listings so that you can target and attract the right audience and clientele to your store. The website also contains a step by step guide on how to make the most on it and give your shop a boost and reach most of its users. More traffic means more opportunities to sell products and make money. Some of the ways in which you can boost your traffic include:

Social Media: you can use platforms like Twitter, Facebook, etc. to promote your online business

SEO: optimising your product listings for search engines will increase the exposure they will get, and will make it easy for potential buyers to find them

Tags: Like categories on Amazon, Etsy uses tags. Tags are just like keywords and make it easier for the potential buyers to find your products. You can use 13 tags for a product.

Growth Potential and Increasing Sales

Though Etsy launched in 2005 and has been around for less than a decade, it has grown exponentially. It is home to more than 800,000 stores and is continuously growing. The website is updated frequently to make its use convenient for both buyers and sellers alike, and in 2011 alone the website saw a 74% increase since 2010. Now that Etsy is easily recognised for artisan and handmade products it offers, it has more potential than ever before, which can be seen in the ever-increasing number of sales and profits.

Support on Etsy

Whether you are starting out new on Etsy or have been around for a long time, you will definitely benefit from the great support it offers. It has a massive online community of people with mutual interests, and you can also connect with them and get support and advice from them. There are different ways in which you can connect with the experts and the experienced on Etsy, and they include:

The live chat and the email support system

Whether you have a question regarding setup or just need some help getting started, you can get support from the Etsy team immediately through their live chat, or you can email them to get your questions answered and problems solved.

Etsy teams that you can join

Etsy has thousands of stores offering different kinds of products, but to make it easier for people with common interests to connect with each other, it introduced teams. You can join the team you like to connect with other people whom you share interests with. There are teams for the manufacturers of specific products, like jewellery designers, clothing designers, etc. It has more than 3000 teams of different genres, so no matter what your genre is, you will find people to connect with. And if your interests are truly unique or you offer something that no one else offers, you can easily create your own genre and invite your friends and fellows to join your team.

People working in teams can not only get advice and suggestions from each other, but they can also collaborate, offer discounts and specials and promote each other's stores.

Participation in its online forums

Another great thing that Etsy offers is its forums. You can get all sorts of ideas, help, feedback, etc. in there, discuss and share ideas, talk to other people and hear their stories, inspire and get inspired, etc. Forums offer endless opportunities for ideas, support, and inspiration.

Cross-Promotion

Whether or not Etsy is your main platform for selling your stuff, you can benefit greatly from it and bring more exposure to your business. People who mainly operate their businesses through their websites also use it to reach a wider audience and bring more exposure to their businesses. Etsy can be utilised in several different ways, some of which include:

- Retail Store

While you can sell your products at a wholesale rate from your website, you can use Etsy to sell your products at the retail prices. This way you will be able to cater to both individual and bulk buyers separately and easily without getting anything mixed up.

- Wholesale Store

Alternatively, you can use Etsy to create a wholesale store, so while you sell items at retail prices from your website, you can sell them in bulk to other retailers from your Etsy store.

Venture Into New Territories

The options with Etsy are endless. If you already have a successful business but would like to venture into a completely new, different, and unrelated territory than the one you are currently involved in, you can use Etsy as your platform to do so. With the easy setup, there will be no hassle and you will be able to test how the new product fares without having to spend too much.

- Multiple Shops

You can have more than one shop on Etsy, so if you want to offer items that fall into different categories, you can create different shops for them. You can also promote your Etsy shops by offering coupons and discounts for purchases on your Etsy store when people buy your products from your website or some other place. The possibilities are utterly endless and it is entirely up to you how you use Etsy. You can have multiple shops and use them to promote one another and reach an even larger audience.

Now that you know what Etsy is and what you can use it for, and understand the benefits of using it, we will move on to how you can make your first $1000 on it without having to spend a dime. But before doing that, you need to learn how to create an account on Etsy, set up your shop, optimise it for search engines, and ensure that your customers are 100% satisfied. Satisfied customers are good for business in several ways: they become loyal and returning customers, and if their experience with you is good, they will spread the word and bring you more traffic. It has been seen that once a customer has a bad experience with you, they are likely to stop buying from you. A satisfied customer is less likely to leave a good review, but a disgruntled and an unhappy customer will most definitely leave you a bad review that can damage your reputation.

Chapter 3 – Creating an Account and Setting up Your Shop on Etsy

In this chapter you will learn how to create an account on Etsy and setup your shop. To make the process easy for you to understand, I will take you through the process step by step.

Creating an Account

Go to etsy.com

On the top right of the screen, click on blue-green register button. A new window will pop up on your screen.

Now you will have two options for registering for an account: (a) Sign up using Facebook, and (b) Sign up using email

If you sign up using Facebook, the email you use for Facebook will be used and the required information will be pulled from Facebook as well.

If you do not want to use Facebook to sign up, you can register using your email address,

For the latter method, enter the required information:

First Name - Enter your real first name

Last Name - Enter your real last name

Gender - Options to choose from include 'Male,' Female,' and 'Rather not say'

Email - Enter the email address you want to register with

Password - Enter the password you want to use

Confirm Password - Retype the password to confirm it

Username - Choose a username

To receive the Etsy newsletter, tick the box next to: *"I want to receive Etsy Finds, an email newsletter of fresh trends and editors' picks."*

Make sure that you enter a secure password that includes both upper case and lower case letters, special characters, as well as numbers. Change your password at least once a month to keep your account fully protected.

Once you enter all the information, register your account. A confirmation email will be sent to your inbox and registration will complete once you confirm it.

Opening Up a Shop

Once you have completed your account registration, you can open your shop on Etsy. To do so, log in to your account and scroll down to the bottom of the page. You will notice a blue-green button under the heading of *'Turn Your Passion Into a Business.'* Click on the button that says, 'Open a Shop.'

When you click on the 'Open a Shop' button, the shop creation setup will start.

The first step is to set a language, currency, and shop country. (It will have a suggestion as well, for faster setup.)

To go with the suggestion, click on 'Yes.' To customise, click on 'No, I want to choose.'

By clicking on the latter, you will have the option to select the language, currency, and the country of your shop.

In the next step, you will be asked to choose what you want to accomplish on Etsy. The options include:

Reach Etsy buyers, I already sell full time

Quit my day job and sell full time

Sell in my spare time

Other

Choose the most relevant option. We are choosing the second one to start our shop.

You will be required to enter a name for your shop. It will appear with your items in the Etsy marketplace, so pick a name that has personal significance or helps identify what's in your shop. You can change the name later if you want.

Then you can start adding items to your shop. The more items you add, the more your chances of getting discovered are. Click on 'List a new item' to start listing.

To list the item, you will have to fill out some information about it, like who the manufacturer of that item is.

Next you have to select a category for your item.

Then you have to select whether the item is digital or physical. Yes, you can sell digital items on Etsy as well. Buyers can download the digital files as soon as the payment is confirmed.

You can also add different properties and variations for your products, like colour, material, flavour, pattern, etc.

Item Title: Then you will have to add a title for your item. The title can have 140 characters. Choose a title that accurately describes your product. Make sure that the title you choose is also a keyword that people use to search for similar items. You can find Etsy's on guide on Search Engine Optimisation here: https://www.etsy.com/storque/media/bunker/2009/09/Etsy_Sellers_Guide_to_SEO_Version_1.0_.pdf

Photos: Then you will have to add the photos. Add different photos so that potential buyers can see the different styles, colours, patterns, materials, etc. of the products. It is very important to take good quality photos. A good photo will appeal to the buyers and increase the chances of your product getting sold, while a bad photo will make the buyers lose interest and decrease the chances of the product getting sold. A good photo is one that gives the buyer an exact idea about what to expect, and accurately conveys the colour, shape, and size of the product. Here's how to take good photos:

Use a good quality camera that can capture the intricate details of the product.

Use natural light to take photos. Make sure that it is not too sunny or dark when you are taking a photo, as the colours will appear different when light is too bright and that may mislead the customers.

Take pictures on clear white or black backgrounds, or any colour that is in contrast with the product so that the product gets the proper spotlight. Also add a picture or two of the product/item in use, if that makes it look better.

Get creative and take photos that actually stand out. When photographing clothes, you can use mannequins or models, and use different combinations and styles to give buyers better styling ideas about your product.

Description: Add a description for your product. The description you add will also be used on Google and other search engines. Make sure to include search engine friendly keywords. You should include at least one keyword in every 100 words of description.

Tags: Tags also work as keywords and make your products easy to discover. You can use up to 13 tags, so use them wisely and carefully. By using the right tags, you ensure that buyers looking for a product like yours will easily be able to find it. Include both specific and general keywords.

Then add the Material, Price, and Quantity of your product.

Then you have to enter the shipping information for your product.

After you have entered all the information, click on 'Preview Listing' to see your product listing.

You will then be able to see how your product will appear to potential customers. From there you can either edit it to make changes, or click on 'Save and Continue' to proceed.

Then follow the setup as it takes you step by step to add your credit card or setup an international payment method, and proceed to open your shop.

Chapter 4 – How to Keep Your Customers Satisfied and Happy

While Etsy is a great platform and will bring genuine buyers to your page, it depends entirely on you whether you keep them or not. A customer will stumble on your page now and then, browse around, find something to buy, but it is the experience they have on your shop that will decide whether or not they will return. Many online stores lose a lot of customers because they fail to keep them happy. Here's how to ensure that your customers remain happy and keep returning.

Stocks

Make sure that the products you offer are always in stock so that you do not have to turn away any customers. Most online stores ship directly from their warehouses, so make sure that the online stock is updated. If your online store lists more products than you have in stock, you will end up disappointing your customers.

Ship on Time

It is really important to ship the products on time. Timely delivery wins customers while untimely delivery damages your reputation badly. You have to understand that your customers have a life and there's a lot more to things that people buy than you will ever know. Sometimes people buy things as presents for others, and timely delivery is really important in those cases. If the customers don't receive the products on time, it will likely cause them unnecessary stress, and no matter how much they like your stuff, they will avoid it and find other places to buy it from. So, deliver on time, as you promise.

Gifts and Freebies

You should treat your regular and returning customers with something special to make them feel special. Try waiving the shipping charges on large orders, offering small discounts, or just sending a sticker or memento along with their order to let them know that they are valued. If they feel special buying items from you, they will be naturally inclined towards buying from you over and again.

Under Promise and Over Deliver

You may be capable of doing a lot more but it is best if you under promise and over deliver. What this means is that your customers will expect less from you and you will continuously exceed their expectations. If you fail to exceed their expectations, it won't be an issue because you under-promised.

Get Back to Them ASAP!

It is very important that you answer all customer queries as soon as you can. Ideally, you should reply to customers within 24 hours during weekdays. Ignoring customers and not solving their issues will likely result in bad and negative reviews for your store.

Become Proactive

Anticipate the needs of your customers and bring solutions. This bodes well with customers because you solve the problems before they become problems, so your customers never get a chance to complain or be unhappy.

Chapter 5 – Start Selling on Etsy without Spending a Dime

In order to make profits by selling items on Etsy without spending a dime, the best way to go is to start by selling items from your home that you do not use. Since Etsy is neither Amazon nor eBay, you can't start by selling old furniture, etc. You need to find artistic and crafty things that have value and that people will be interested in buying.

Dig Out Old Stuff

Look at the old clothes; find stuff that is over 20 years old. You may find some vintage buttons, special edition sew-on buttons, etc. This is the type of stuff that sells on Etsy. Hipsters are always on the lookout for vintage clothing items, and if you find those, you are in luck! If you dig up in the attic, you will likely find a vintage item that is in good condition, something you have no interest in, something that people will pay handsomely for. Gothic and grungy items are also popular among hipsters and will sell easily.

It is entirely up to you what you want to sell. You can even put up old toys, limited edition figures and figurines, Legos, etc. for sale. Anything that is no longer produced has a certain value attached to it. If you find collector items, like buttons, coins, etc., then you can list them and sell them too. If you have old paintings, sculptures, etc., then you can list those as well. At this stage, our main goal is to sell products and items that are of good quality, are valuable, and are already available at home, but happen to be things we do not need. By selling them, you can start earning money without having spent a dime. Later on, you can use this money as investment and venture into a new territory. Jewellery is also very popular on Etsy, especially custom designs, so that is another thing you can invest in.

In the next chapter, we will discuss the items that are popular and sell well on Etsy. Once you have earned enough from the items you already had, you can move on and find other things to sell.

Chapter 6 – Things that Sell Well on Etsy

Etsy does not allow reselling of items so you will have to find something unique to invest your money in. For instance, you can start going to garage sales to scavenge vintage and worthy items that you can buy at cheap rates and sell for more on your Etsy shop. To appeal to your customers you need to be different and offer something that others do not offer. If you are into sewing and designing then there is a lot more you can put your skills to for making money.

Custom Items

Custom items have always appealed to people and sell well. If you start offering customised items to people, you will be giving them something truly unique, like a photo painted on a shirt, on a mug, etc., because these happen to be things that they will not be able to get from anywhere else. For instance, you can buy a shirt at a store, but you can't get a shirt with your photo handprinted on it, can you? By offering these custom items, you can create your own brand and not only become unique but make your customers feel unique too.

Paintings

Artists can sell their arts on Etsy. It is an excellent platform where collectors can get your paintings from you. Limited edition items also sell well because people jump at every opportunity to get their hands on things that will only have limited copies.

Clothes

One of the main items sold by a shop that ranks among the top 5 shops on Etsy are clothes. The custom designed clothes include shirts, t-shirts, vintage shirts, hoodies, etc. Custom warmers, socks, knit scarves, etc. are also among the popular items.

Hand-Made and Children's Items

Handmade items are also unique and therefore among the top selling crafts on Etsy. You can also lure in parents by offering custom made clothes, hair bands, etc. for babies, toddlers, and children. They make excellent gifts and are also among the best sellers.

Vinyl Stickers, Buttons, etc.

Vinyl stickers, buttons, and basically anything that people can't get elsewhere is what you should sell on

Etsy. You can design custom photo frames, cushion covers, bed sheets, embroidered items, etc. and list them on your store. You can even promote your own culture internationally because the audience you will have on Etsy will be the whole world.

These, though, are just a few examples. There is no limit to creativity and arts or what you can do with it, and, therefore, there can't be a list that lists everything you can or should sell on Etsy. You can buy DIY sewing, jewellery, or even glass painting kits and start making items to sell on your shop. Just remember to price your items reasonably to boost your sales. Items priced between $3 and $25 sell easily, while items that cost more do not sell so easily, but of course, if you put in a lot of work, you should charge accordingly.

32

Conclusion

Thank you again for downloading this book!

I hope this book was able to help you become successful on Etsy.

The next step is to venture into new territories and fully realise your entrepreneurial potential.

Finally, if you enjoyed this book, then I'd like to ask you for a favor, would you be kind enough to leave a review for this book on Amazon? It'd be greatly appreciated!

Click here to leave a review for this book on Amazon!

http://amzn.to/1xVmOUj

Thank you and good luck!

Check Out My Other Books

Below you'll find some of my other popular books that are popular on Amazon and Kindle as well. Simply click on the links below to check them out.

SEO Basics: How to use Search Engine Optimization (SEO) to take your business to the next level of success

Social Media Marketing for Beginners: How to build a social media strategy that really works

Affiliate Marketing for Beginners: Simple, smart and proven strategies to make A LOT of money online, the easy way

If the links do not work, for whatever reason, you can simply search for these titles on the Amazon website to find them.

© Copyright 2014 - All rights reserved.

This document is geared towards providing exact and reliable information in regards to the topic and issue covered. The publication is sold with the idea that the publisher is not required to render accounting, officially permitted, or otherwise, qualified services. If advice is necessary, legal or professional, a practiced individual in the profession should be ordered.

- From a Declaration of Principles which was accepted and approved equally by a Committee of the American Bar Association and a Committee of Publishers and Associations.

In no way is it legal to reproduce, duplicate, or transmit any part of this document in either electronic means or in printed format. Recording of this publication is strictly prohibited and any storage of this document is not allowed unless with written permission from the publisher. All rights reserved.

The information provided herein is stated to be truthful and consistent, in that any liability, in terms of inattention or otherwise, by any usage or abuse of any policies, processes, or directions contained within is the solitary and utter responsibility of the recipient reader. Under no circumstances will any legal responsibility or blame be held against the publisher for any reparation, damages, or monetary loss due to the information herein, either directly or indirectly.

Respective authors own all copyrights not held by the publisher.

The information herein is offered for informational purposes solely, and is universal as so. The presentation of the information is without contract or any type of guarantee assurance.

The trademarks that are used are without any consent, and the publication of the trademark is without permission or backing by the trademark owner. All trademarks and brands within this book are for clarifying purposes only and are the owned by the owners themselves, not affiliated with this document.

www.ingramcontent.com/pod-product-compliance
Lightning Source LLC
Chambersburg PA
CBHW051824170526
45167CB00005B/2147